Greetings FROM
Florida

Greetings FROM
Florida

Greetings FROM
Florida

Greetings FROM
Florida

Greetings FROM
Florida

Greetings FROM
Florida

Greetings FROM
Florida

Greetings FROM
Florida

Greetings FROM
Florida

Greetings FROM
Florida

Greetings FROM
Florida

Greetings FROM
Florida

Greetings FROM
Florida

Greetings FROM
Florida

Greetings FROM
Florida

Greetings FROM
FORT LAUDERDALE
Florida

Greetings FROM
Florida

Greetings FROM
Florida

Greetings FROM
Florida

Greetings FROM
Florida

Greetings FROM
Florida

Greetings FROM
Florida

Greetings FROM
Florida

Greetings FROM
Florida

Greetings FROM
Florida

Greetings FROM
Florida

Greetings FROM
Florida

Greetings FROM
Florida

Greetings FROM
Florida

Greetings FROM
Florida

Greetings FROM
Florida

Greetings FROM
Florida

Greetings FROM
Florida

Greetings FROM
FORT LAUDERDALE
Florida

Greetings FROM
Florida

Greetings FROM
Florida

Greetings FROM
Florida

Greetings FROM
Florida

Greetings FROM
Florida

Greetings FROM
Florida

Greetings FROM
FORT LAUDERDALE
Florida

Greetings FROM
Florida

Greetings FROM
Florida

Greetings FROM
Florida

Greetings FROM
Florida

Greetings FROM
Florida

Greetings FROM
Florida

Greetings FROM
Florida

Greetings FROM
Florida

Greetings FROM
Florida

Greetings FROM
Florida

Greetings FROM
Florida

Greetings FROM
Florida

Greetings FROM
Florida

Greetings FROM
Florida

Greetings FROM
Florida

Greetings FROM
Florida

Greetings FROM
Florida

Greetings FROM
Florida

Greetings FROM
Florida

Greetings FROM
Florida

Greetings FROM
Florida

Greetings FROM
Florida

Greetings FROM
Florida

Greetings FROM
Florida

Greetings FROM
Florida

Greetings FROM
Florida

Greetings FROM
Florida

Greetings FROM
Florida

Greetings FROM
FORT LAUDERDALE
Florida

Greetings FROM
Florida

Greetings FROM
Florida

Greetings FROM
Florida

Greetings FROM
Florida

Greetings FROM
Florida

Printed in the USA
CPSIA information can be obtained
at www.ICGtesting.com
LVHW091144120724
785323LV00003B/153

9 798385 409921